writing workbook companion
for Teach Your Child to Read
in 100 Easy Lessons

writing workbook companion

for

Teach Your Child to Read in 100 Easy Lessons
Revised and Updated Second Edition

Boost Publishing

Please Note: This is a writing companion workbook based on the book *Teach Your Child to Read in 100 Easy Lessons: Revised and Updated Second Edition* by Siegfried Engelmann, et al. This workbook is not affiliated to nor endorsed by the original book or author in any way. If you have not yet purchased the original book, please do so before using this companion guide as this book is meant to enhance your experience, not replace the original work.

Introduction

Are you ready to embark on an exciting journey to teach your child to read? If you haven't gotten your hands on *Teach Your Child to Read in 100 Easy Lessons: Revised and Updated Second Edition* by Siegfried Engelmann, et al, **STOP HERE**. Run, don't walk(!) and pick up a copy today because this book is the only one you'll need to teach your child to read. That and this workbook, of course.

In the original book, each of the 100 lessons is carefully crafted to guide your child through the process of learning to read, with tasks designed to reinforce their understanding. Towards the end of each lesson, there's a crucial writing task—transferring the sounds and letters learned onto a separate sheet of paper while referencing the "sound writing chart" in the beginning of the book.

While the writing component in each lesson is critical for learning, the original process is tedious and requires a great deal of extra effort, time and materials, while also opening up the door for errors.

Enter this Writing Workbook Companion, your one-stop solution to save time and make the process smoother for both you and your reader.

Each page in this workbook is dedicated to a specific lesson, mirroring the sequence of the original book. It's a seamless companion, eliminating the need for separate materials and constant flipping back and forth.

Included in this workbook, you'll find:

√ 100 individual writing lessons that correspond to each of the 100 lessons in the original *Teach Your Child to Read in 100 Easy Lessons*

√ Comprehensive sound-writing instructions for each sound/letter along with practice lines for each lesson. (No need for extra materials as everything is included)

√ Tips & Tricks to ensure a successful and tear-free reading journey

√ Interactive reward chart to track your child's progress, boost their confidence and motivate them to keep working

√ Graduation "certificate" celebrating the child's completion of their 100 lessons

√ Additional writing space for extra practice

With that, let's dive in, celebrate each step, and watch your child blossom into a confident reader!

A letter from the author

Dear amazing (and probably exhausted) caregiver-

You have this workbook in your possession because there is a child in your life that you truly care about. Maybe they have an earlier-than-usual interest in reading or maybe they need an extra boost outside of what they are learning in school. No matter the reason, you have chosen to offer up your valuable (and no doubt limited) time to help that child in their reading journey. Cheers to you!

I, too, am an exhausted human being that cares deeply about my own children. When I first purchased Siegfried Engelmann's book for my 4 year old daughter, I jumped in with stars in my eyes and great plans for my budding reader. But...when we actually started the lessons, I realized that this journey was going to require A LOT of time, energy and patience from the both of us.

As you'll see in the original book, each lesson concludes with a writing module to help the child grasp their own understanding of how to write the sounds/letters they are learning to read. As you can imagine, this step is critical; however, the original book required many additional steps to complete the lesson and outside materials that weren't always available.

As I was going through the lessons with my daughter, I found myself dreading (and sometimes skipping--shhh!) the writing task as it required so much extra effort. I longed for an easier way with simple instructions and readily available templates. Hence, this workbook was born.

My goal is to eliminate as many barriers as possible for you during this process to help make your reading journey a success. I included some tips/tricks that I found helpful as well as some additional tools to make this a positive experience for both you and your reader.

I sincerely hope this workbook helps make things a bit easier.

Sending you so much love (and patience).

Ariana Lawrence, Mom & CEO of Boost Publishing

Tips & tricks for success

Consistency is Key

Do your best to create an environment and structure that promotes consistent practice and exposure to learning.

- Designate a time each day that works for you and your reader. Pick a time that will set you up for success and try to maintain that same time each day.
- Create a special area where you can practice the lessons, ideally free from distractions.
- Try to stick to consecutive days, even if you only get through a couple minutes of the lesson. Too many missed days slows progress (trust me).

Make it Fun

The idea is to foster a love for learning and reading. Create a playful environment to make the process enjoyable.

- Turn reading lessons into a game where the child earns points, stickers or high fives
- Incorporate silly words using the sounds you learned or have a dance party between modules
- Make a game, song or puppet show or draw a picture together of themes you learned in each lesson

Keep it Light

Try to maintain a relaxed and positive atmosphere during reading sessions to help prevent stress and encourage your child to keep going.

- If your reader is too tired or having an "off day", that's ok. Recognize that some days are tough and try again tomorrow.
- Don't be afraid to pause, go slow, or bookmark a lesson until the next day.
- Normalize mistakes and remind the child that they are a part of the process.

Tips & tricks for success

Praise Progress

Celebrate small victories and milestones along the way. Positive reinforcement can boost your child's confidence and motivation to continue learning.

- Applaud your child for trying to sound out a new word, regardless of whether they get it right or wrong.
- Use the star chart in this workbook to record and reward progress or create your own reward system.
- Use praise that encourages a growth mindset: ex. "You worked so hard today", "You should be so proud of how much you've been practicing" and "I can see how much you're focusing".

Be Patient and Supportive

Learning to read is a process that requires time, patience, and gentle guidance.

- Offer words of encouragement when the child struggles, reassuring them that it's okay to take their time.
- Model patience by calmly assisting the child when they get frustrated or lose focus during lessons, showing them that mistakes are a natural part of learning.
- Pay attention to your child's disposition each day and adjust the lesson tone & timing to accommodate their needs.

Give Yourself Grace

Let's face it, this process can be tough on the teacher too. Be kind to yourself along the way.

- Forgive yourself if you need to miss a day; simply pick up where you left off the next day.
- Don't be too hard on yourself if a certain teaching method doesn't work as expected; instead, try different approaches until you find what resonates with your child.
- Remember to take breaks and recharge when needed, prioritizing your own well-being so you can continue to support your child effectively.
- Do what works for you and don't do what feels too hard. Celebrate yourself and your small wins too. You're doing great!

Star chart

Included in this workbook is an optional star chart, ready and waiting to be personalized with your child's name. It's all about celebrating progress and effort rather than just focusing on the skill of reading.

After each lesson, your child can jazz up their star chart by coloring or checking off the stars that match what they've accomplished. It's included on the next page for easy access.

You've got options on how to use it: You can either tear out these pages and hang them up somewhere your child can see them every day, or you can keep them tucked away in the workbook to track progress there.

Depending on your child and/or your own personal values, you may want to incorporate additional rewards. Some parents have found a little treat after each lesson works wonders—a piece of candy, a bit of bonus playtime, or maybe even a coin in the ol' piggy bank.

Ideas

Then, there's the medium-sized stuff, like a little prize after 10 lessons or completing a row on the chart—think dollar store goodies, an extra playdate with pals, or a trinket from the treasure chest.

And for the grand finale, there's the big reward for finishing the whole workbook —like snagging that special toy they've been eyeing, planning an awesome activity together, or picking out a stack of new books to enjoy with their newfound reading skills.

The key here is finding what aligns with your family values, what fits into your routine, and what really lights a fire under your child to keep at it. So, go on, make it your own adventure and have a bit of fun!

_____'s reading chart

11

Let's begin

The next section corresponds to each lesson in *Teach Your Child to Read in 100 Easy Lessons: Revised and Updated Second Edition* by Siegfried Engelmann, et al. Once you get to the last task in each lesson in Engelmann's book, switch over to this workbook for the corresponding writing task. Enjoy and happy learning!

Lesson 1: Task 6
Writing the sound m

Now we're going to practice writing the sound you learned.

To write the sound "m", start at the dot at the top and draw a line down, then go back to the top and make two humps.

start here m

Watch me trace the mmm sound. Trace the mmm sound.
Next, it's your turn to trace the mmm sound and write some of your own.

m m m

m

Fun tip: Tell your child you're going to "circle" your favorite mmm that they wrote. Tell them why you chose it.

Lesson 2: Task 7
Writing sounds s and m

Now we're going to practice writing the sounds you learned.

To write the sound "s", start at the top and make a curve to the left and curve down the other way all the way down.

s start here

Watch me trace the sss sound. Trace the sss sound.
Next, it's your turn to trace the sss sound and write some of your own.

s   s   s

s

Now, watch me trace the mmm sound. Trace the mmm sound.
Next, it's your turn to trace the mmm sound and write some of your own.

m   m   m

m

Lesson 3: Task 8
Writing sounds a and m

Now we're going to practice writing the sounds you learned.

To write the sound "a", start at the dot and make a circle to the left. Slide up to create the vertical line and draw straight back down to complete the "tail".

a start here

Watch me trace the aaa sound. Trace the aaa sound.
Next, it's your turn to trace the aaa sound and write some of your own.

a ⠁ ⠁

⠁

Now, watch me trace the mmm sound. Trace the mmm sound.
Next, it's your turn to trace the mmm sound and write some of your own.

m ⠍ ⠍

⠍

Lesson 4: Task 7
Writing sounds s and a

Now we're going to practice writing the sounds you learned.

Watch me trace the sss sound. Trace the sss sound.
Next, it's your turn to trace the sss sound and write some of your own.

s s s

s

Now, watch me trace the aaa sound. Trace the aaa sound.
Next, it's your turn to trace the aaa sound and write some of your own.

a a a

a

Lesson 5: Task 9
Writing sounds ē and a

Now we're going to practice writing the sounds you learned.

Let's start by writing the ēēē sound without the line. To write the sound "ēēē", start at the dot and make horizontal line to the right. Curve to the left and make a "c" around it.

start here  **Note:** Do not make the line over the **e**

Watch me trace the ēēē sound. Trace the ēēē sound.
Next, it's your turn to trace the ēēē sound and write some of your own.

Now, watch me trace the aaa sound. Trace the aaa sound.
Next, it's your turn to trace the aaa sound and write some of your own.

17

Fun tip: Tell your child you're going to "circle" your favorite eee and aaa that they wrote. Tell them why you chose it.

Lesson 6: Task 8
Writing sounds ē and s

Now we're going to practice writing the sounds you learned.

Watch me trace the ēēē sound. Trace the ēēē sound. **Note:** Do not make the line over the **e**.
Next, it's your turn to trace the ēēē sound and write some of your own.

Now, watch me trace the sss sound. Trace the sss sound.
Next, it's your turn to trace the sss sound and write some of your own.

Lesson 7: Task 9
Writing sounds t and m

Now we're going to practice writing the sounds you learned.

To write the sound "t", start at the dot at the top and make a straight line down. Release your pencil and cross the line in the middle.

Note: Point out to the child this sound takes up the whole line space instead of just the bottom.

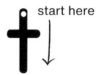
start here

Watch me trace the t sound. Trace the t sound.
Next, it's your turn to trace the t sound and write some of your own.

Now, watch me trace the mmm sound. Trace the mmm sound.
Next, it's your turn to trace the mmm sound and write some of your own.

Lesson 8: Task 8
Writing sounds s and t

Now we're going to practice writing the sounds you learned.

Watch me trace the sss sound. Trace the sss sound.
Next, it's your turn to trace the sss sound and write some of your own.

S s s

s

Now, watch me trace the t sound. Trace the t sound.
Next, it's your turn to trace the t sound and write some of your own.

t t t

t

Lesson 9: Task 13
Writing sounds r and a

Now we're going to practice writing the sounds you learned.

To write the sound "r", start at the dot and make a straight line down. Then come back up the line and make a curve to the right.

Watch me trace the rrr sound. Trace the rrr sound.
Next, it's your turn to trace the r sound and write some of your own.

Now, watch me trace the aaa sound. Trace the aaa sound.
Next, it's your turn to trace the aaa sound and write some of your own.

Lesson 10: Task 12
Writing sounds r and a

Now we're going to practice writing the sounds you learned.

Watch me trace the rrr sound. Trace the rrr sound.
Next, it's your turn to trace the rrr sound and write some of your own.

r r r

r

Now, watch me trace the aaa sound. Trace the aaa sound.
Next, it's your turn to trace the aaa sound and write some of your own.

a a a

a

Lesson 11: Task 9
Writing sounds t and ē

Now we're going to practice writing the sounds you learned.

Watch me trace the t sound. Trace the t sound.
Next, it's your turn to trace the t sound and write some of your own.

Watch me trace the ēēē sound. Trace the ēēē sound. **Note:** Do not make the line over the **e**.
Next, it's your turn to trace the ēēē sound and write some of your own.

Lesson 12: Task 9
Writing sounds d and a

Now we're going to practice writing the sounds you learned.

To write the sound "d", start at the dot and make a "c". Keeping your pencil on the paper, make a vertical line straight up, then trace the vertical line straight down again to make the "tail".

start here

Note: Point out to the child this sound takes up the whole line space instead of just the bottom.

Watch me trace the d sound. Trace the d sound.
Next, it's your turn to trace the d sound and write some of your own.

Now, watch me trace the aaa sound. Trace the aaa sound.
Next, it's your turn to trace the aaa sound and write some of your own.

Remember: There are extra lined sheets in the back of the workbook if you need more space for practice.

Lesson 13: Task 11
Writing sounds s and d

Now we're going to practice writing the sounds you learned.

Watch me trace the sss sound. Trace the sss sound.
Next, it's your turn to trace the sss sound and write some of your own.

s s s

s

Now, watch me trace the d sound. Trace the d sound.
Next, it's your turn to trace the d sound and write some of your own.

d d d

d

Lesson 14: Task 11
Writing sounds i and ē

Now we're going to practice writing the sounds you learned.

To write the sound "i", start at the dot on the middle line and draw a vertical line straight down. Lift your pencil and add a dot.

start here **i** ↓

Watch me trace the iii sound. Trace the iii sound.
Next, it's your turn to trace the iii sound and write some of your own.

Watch me trace the ēēē sound. Trace the ēēē sound. **Note:** Do not make the line over the **e**.
Next, it's your turn to trace the ēēē sound and write some of your own.

Lesson 15: Task 10
Writing sounds r and t

Now we're going to practice writing the sounds you learned.

Watch me trace the rrr sound. Trace the rrr sound.
Next, it's your turn to trace the rrr sound and write some of your own.

Now, watch me trace the t sound. Trace the t sound.
Next, it's your turn to trace the t sound and write some of your own.

Lesson 16: Task 11
Writing sounds d and i

Now we're going to practice writing the sounds you learned.

Watch me trace the d sound. Trace the d sound.
Next, it's your turn to trace the d sound and write some of your own.

Watch me trace the iii sound. Trace the iii sound.
Next, it's your turn to trace the iii sound and write some of your own.

Lesson 17: Task 10
Writing sounds s and ē

Now we're going to practice writing the sounds you learned.

Watch me trace the sss sound. Trace the sss sound.
Next, it's your turn to trace the sss sound and write some of your own.

Watch me trace the ēēē sound. Trace the ēēē sound. **Note:** Do not make the line over the **e**.
Next, it's your turn to trace the ēēē sound and write some of your own.

Lesson 18: Task 10
Writing sounds m and a

Now we're going to practice writing the sounds you learned.

Watch me trace the mmm sound. Trace the mmm sound.
Next, it's your turn to trace the mmm sound and write some of your own.

m m m m

m

Now, watch me trace the aaa sound. Trace the aaa sound.
Next, it's your turn to trace the aaa sound and write some of your own.

a a a

a

Lesson 19: Task 12
Writing sounds d and r

Now we're going to practice writing the sounds you learned.

Watch me trace the d sound. Trace the d sound.
Next, it's your turn to trace the d sound and write some of your own.

Watch me trace the rrr sound. Trace the rrr sound.
Next, it's your turn to trace the rrr sound and write some of your own.

Lesson 20: Task 11
Writing sounds c and d

Now we're going to practice writing the sounds you learned.

To write the sound "c", start at the dot and curve around to make a semi-circle.

 start here

Watch me trace the c sound. Trace the c sound.
Next, it's your turn to trace the c sound and write some of your own.

Now, watch me trace the d sound. Trace the d sound.
Next, it's your turn to trace the d sound and write some of your own.

Lesson 21: Task 11
Writing sounds i and t

Now we're going to practice writing the sounds you learned.

Watch me trace the iii sound. Trace the iii sound.
Next, it's your turn to trace the iii sound and write some of your own.

Now, watch me trace the t sound. Trace the t sound.
Next, it's your turn to trace the t sound and write some of your own.

Lesson 22: Task 10
Writing sounds o and c

Now we're going to practice writing the sounds you learned.

To write the sound "o", start at the dot and curve like you're making a "c", then close to make a full circle.

start here

Watch me trace the ooo sound. Trace the ooo sound.
Next, it's your turn to trace the ooo sound and write some of your own.

Now, watch me trace the c sound. Trace the c sound.
Next, it's your turn to trace the c sound and write some of your own.

Lesson 23: Task 11
Writing sounds r and o

Now we're going to practice writing the sounds you learned.

Watch me trace the rrr sound. Trace the rrr sound.
Next, it's your turn to trace the rrr sound and write some of your own.

Now, watch me trace the ooo sound. Trace the ooo sound.
Next, it's your turn to trace the ooo sound and write some of your own.

Lesson 24: Task 10
Writing sounds n and d

Now we're going to practice writing the sounds you learned.

To write the sound "n", start at the dot on the top and draw a line down, then go back to the top and make one hump.

start here | n

Tip: It's just like making the mmm sound but stop at one hump, instead of two.

Watch me trace the nnn sound. Trace the nnn sound.
Next, it's your turn to trace the nnn sound and write some of your own.

n n n

n

Now, watch me trace the d sound. Trace the d sound.
Next, it's your turn to trace the d sound and write some of your own.

d d d

d

Lesson 25: Task 10
Writing sounds n and o

Now we're going to practice writing the sounds you learned.

Watch me trace the nnn sound. Trace the nnn sound.
Next, it's your turn to trace the nnn sound and write some of your own.

n n n

n

Now, watch me trace the ooo sound. Trace the ooo sound.
Next, it's your turn to trace the ooo sound and write some of your own.

o o o

o

Lesson 26: Task 9
Writing sounds f and s

Now we're going to practice writing the sounds you learned.

To write the sound "f", start at the dot slightly below the top line and create a "cane" to the left and down. Lift your pencil and cross the "cane" at the center line.

Note: Point out to the child this sound takes up the whole line space instead of just the bottom.

start here

Watch me trace the fff sound. Trace the fff sound.
Next, it's your turn to trace the fff sound and write some of your own.

f f f

f

Now, watch me trace the sss sound. Trace the sss sound.
Next, it's your turn to trace the sss sound and write some of your own.

s s s

s

Lesson 27: Task 11
Writing sounds o and c

Now we're going to practice writing the sounds you learned.

Watch me trace the ooo sound. Trace the ooo sound.
Next, it's your turn to trace the ooo sound and write some of your own.

Now, watch me trace the c sound. Trace the c sound.
Next, it's your turn to trace the c sound and write some of your own.

Lesson 28: Task 10
Writing sounds n and $\bar{e}$

Now we're going to practice writing the sounds you learned.

Watch me trace the nnn sound. Trace the nnn sound.
Next, it's your turn to trace the nnn sound and write some of your own.

n n n

n

Watch me trace the $\bar{e}\bar{e}\bar{e}$ sound. Trace the $\bar{e}\bar{e}\bar{e}$ sound. **Note:** Do not make the line over the **e**.
Next, it's your turn to trace the $\bar{e}\bar{e}\bar{e}$ sound and write some of your own.

e e e

e

Lesson 29: Task 11
Writing sounds u and n

Now we're going to practice writing the sounds you learned.

To write the sound "u", start at the dot and draw a vertical line down. Create a curve at the bottom and draw up the other side. Once at the top, draw a vertical line down straight to form the "tail".

start here ↓ u

Watch me trace the uuu sound. Trace the uuu sound.
Next, it's your turn to trace the uuu sound and write some of your own.

u u u

u

Now, watch me trace the nnn sound. Trace the nnn sound.
Next, it's your turn to trace the nnn sound and write some of your own.

n n n

n

Lesson 30: Task 10
Writing sounds u and f

Now we're going to practice writing the sounds you learned.

Watch me trace the uuu sound. Trace the uuu sound.
Next, it's your turn to trace the uuu sound and write some of your own.

u u u

u

Now, watch me trace the fff sound. Trace the fff sound.
Next, it's your turn to trace the fff sound and write some of your own.

f f f

f

Lesson 31: Task 13
Writing sounds l and m

Now we're going to practice writing the sounds you learned.

To write the sound "l", start at the dot and draw a vertical line straight down.

Note: Point out to the child this sound takes up the whole line space instead of just the bottom.

start here

Watch me trace the lll sound. Trace the lll sound.
Next, it's your turn to trace the lll sound and write some of your own.

Now, watch me trace the mmm sound. Trace the mmm sound.
Next, it's your turn to trace the mmm sound and write some of your own.

Lesson 32: Task 12
Writing sounds o and t

Now we're going to practice writing the sounds you learned.

Watch me trace the ooo sound. Trace the ooo sound.
Next, it's your turn to trace the ooo sound and write some of your own.

Now, watch me trace the t sound. Trace the t sound.
Next, it's your turn to trace the t sound and write some of your own.

Lesson 33: Task 13
Writing sounds a and f

Now we're going to practice writing the sounds you learned.

Watch me trace the aaa sound. Trace the aaa sound.
Next, it's your turn to trace the aaa sound and write some of your own.

Now, watch me trace the fff sound. Trace the fff sound.
Next, it's your turn to trace the fff sound and write some of your own.

Lesson 34: Task 14
Writing sounds g and c

Now we're going to practice writing the sounds you learned.

To write the sound "g", start at the dot and curve like you're making a "c". Keeping your pencil on the paper, make a vertical line straight up, then trace the vertical line straight down past the bottom line to make a curve.

g start here

Note: Point out to the child this sound's "tail" dips below the bottom line.

Watch me trace the g sound. Trace the g sound.
Next, it's your turn to trace the g sound and write some of your own.

g g g

g

Now, watch me trace the c sound. Trace the c sound.
Next, it's your turn to trace the c sound and write some of your own.

c c c

c

Lesson 35: Task 13
Writing sounds g and d

Now we're going to practice writing the sounds you learned.

Watch me trace the g sound. Trace the g sound.
Next, it's your turn to trace the g sound and write some of your own.

g g g

g

Now, watch me trace the d sound. Trace the d sound.
Next, it's your turn to trace the d sound and write some of your own.

d d d

d

Lesson 36: Task 11
Writing sounds s and u

Now we're going to practice writing the sounds you learned.

Watch me trace the sss sound. Trace the sss sound.
Next, it's your turn to trace the sss sound and write some of your own.

s s s

s

Now, watch me trace the uuu sound. Trace the uuu sound.
Next, it's your turn to trace the uuu sound and write some of your own.

u u u

u

Lesson 37: Task 12
Writing sounds f and g

Now we're going to practice writing the sounds you learned.

Watch me trace the fff sound. Trace the fff sound.
Next, it's your turn to trace the fff sound and write some of your own.

Now, watch me trace the g sound. Trace the g sound.
Next, it's your turn to trace the g sound and write some of your own.

Lesson 38: Task 10
Writing sounds i and u

Now we're going to practice writing the sounds you learned.

Watch me trace the iii sound. Trace the iii sound.
Next, it's your turn to trace the iii sound and write some of your own.

i i i

i

Now, watch me trace the uuu sound. Trace the uuu sound.
Next, it's your turn to trace the uuu sound and write some of your own.

u u u

u

Lesson 39: Task 12
Writing sounds o and m

Now we're going to practice writing the sounds you learned.

Watch me trace the ooo sound. Trace the ooo sound.
Next, it's your turn to trace the ooo sound and write some of your own.

Now, watch me trace the mmm sound. Trace the mmm sound.
Next, it's your turn to trace the mmm sound and write some of your own.

Lesson 40: Task 11
Writing sounds h, d and a

Now we're going to practice writing the sounds you learned.

To write the sound "h", start at the dot and draw a vertical line straight down. Come back up the line halfway and make one hump.

start here

Note: Point out to the child this sound takes up the whole line space instead of just the bottom.

Watch me trace the h sound. Trace the h sound.
Next, it's your turn to trace the h sound and write some of your own.

Now, watch me trace the d sound. Trace the d sound.
Next, it's your turn to trace the d sound and write some of your own.

Lesson 40: Task 12 (continued)

Watch me trace the aaa sound. Trace the aaa sound.
Next, it's your turn to trace the aaa sound and write some of your own.

Lesson 41: Task 11
Writing sounds m and h

Now we're going to practice writing the sounds you learned.

Watch me trace the mmm sound. Trace the mmm sound.
Next, it's your turn to trace the mmm sound and write some of your own.

m m m

m

Now, watch me trace the h sound. Trace the h sound.
Next, it's your turn to trace the h sound and write some of your own.

h h h

h

Lesson 42: Task 10
Writing sounds k and f

Now we're going to practice writing the sounds you learned.

To write the sound "k", start at the dot and draw a vertical line straight down. Pick up your pencil and, from the center line, draw a sideways "v".

Note: Point out to the child this sound takes up the whole line space instead of just the bottom.

Watch me trace the k sound. Trace the k sound.
Next, it's your turn to trace the k sound and write some of your own.

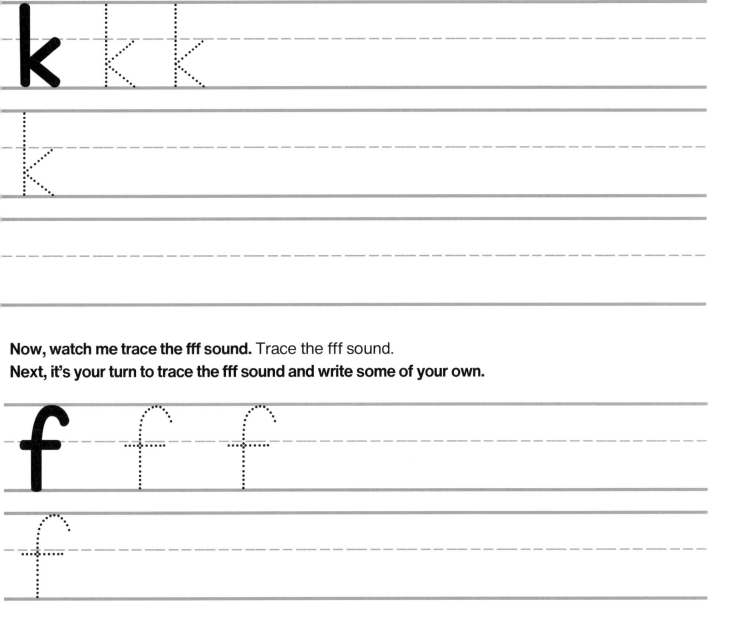

Now, watch me trace the fff sound. Trace the fff sound.
Next, it's your turn to trace the fff sound and write some of your own.

Lesson 43: Task 9
Writing sounds n and h

Now we're going to practice writing the sounds you learned.

Watch me trace the nnn sound. Trace the nnn sound.
Next, it's your turn to trace the nnn sound and write some of your own.

n n n n

n

Now, watch me trace the h sound. Trace the h sound.
Next, it's your turn to trace the h sound and write some of your own.

h h h h

h

Lesson 44: Task 7
Writing sounds o and k

Now we're going to practice writing the sounds you learned.

Watch me trace the ooo sound. Trace the ooo sound.
Next, it's your turn to trace the ooo sound and write some of your own.

Now, watch me trace the k sound. Trace the k sound.
Next, it's your turn to trace the k sound and write some of your own.

Lesson 45: Task 8
Writing sounds k and g

Now we're going to practice writing the sounds you learned.

Watch me trace the k sound. Trace the k sound.
Next, it's your turn to trace the k sound and write some of your own.

k k k

k

Now, watch me trace the g sound. Trace the g sound.
Next, it's your turn to trace the g sound and write some of your own.

g g g

g

Lesson 46: Task 10
Writing sounds v and h

Now we're going to practice writing the sounds you learned.

To write the sound "v", start at the dot and draw a vertical line down diagonally. Come back up the other side until you reach the middle line.

start here

V

Watch me trace the vvv sound. Trace the vvv sound.
Next, it's your turn to trace the vvv sound and write some of your own.

Now, watch me trace the h sound. Trace the h sound.
Next, it's your turn to trace the h sound and write some of your own.

Lesson 47: Task 9
Writing sounds s, h and v

Now we're going to practice writing the sounds you learned.

Watch me trace the sss sound. Trace the sss sound.
Next, it's your turn to trace the sss sound and write some of your own.

s s s

s

Now, watch me trace the h sound. Trace the h sound.
Next, it's your turn to trace the h sound and write some of your own.

h h h

h

Lesson 47: Task 9 (continued)

Watch me trace the vvv sound. Trace the vvv sound.
Next, it's your turn to trace the vvv sound and write some of your own.

V V V

V

Lesson 48: Task 11
Writing sounds w and v

Now we're going to practice writing the sounds you learned.

To write the sound "w", start at the dot and draw a vertical line down diagonally. Come back up the other side until you reach the middle line. Repeat.

start here

W

Tip: It's just like making the vvv sound two times.

Watch me trace the www sound. Trace the www sound.
Next, it's your turn to trace the www sound and write some of your own.

W W W

W

Now, watch me trace the vvv sound. Trace the vvv sound.
Next, it's your turn to trace the vvv sound and write some of your own.

V V V

V

Lesson 49: Task 10
Writing sounds th and sh

Now we're going to practice writing the sounds you learned.

Watch me trace the ththth sound. Trace the ththth sound.
Next, it's your turn to trace the ththth sound and write some of your own.

Tip: The ththth sound uses the t sound and the h sound that we already learned to write. Let's put them together.

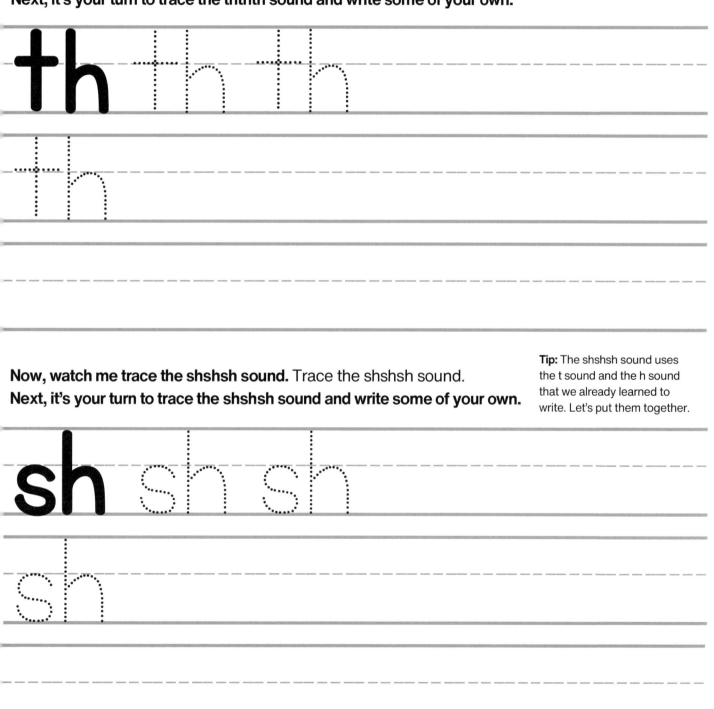

Now, watch me trace the shshsh sound. Trace the shshsh sound.
Next, it's your turn to trace the shshsh sound and write some of your own.

Tip: The shshsh sound uses the t sound and the h sound that we already learned to write. Let's put them together.

Lesson 50: Task 11
Writing sounds w and th

Now we're going to practice writing the sounds you learned.

Watch me trace the www sound. Trace the www sound.
Next, it's your turn to trace the www sound and write some of your own.

W w w

w

Now, watch me trace the ththth sound. Trace the ththth sound.
Next, it's your turn to trace the ththth sound and write some of your own.

th th th

th

Lesson 51: Task 10
Writing sounds p and th

Now we're going to practice writing the sounds you learned.

To write the sound "p", start at the dot on the middle line and draw a straight line down vertically past the bottom line. Lift your pencil and draw a backwards "c" to the right of the line.

Note: Point out to the child this sound's "tail" dips below the bottom line.

Watch me trace the p sound. Trace the p sound.

Next, it's your turn to trace the p sound and write some of your own.

Now, watch me trace the ththth sound. Trace the ththth sound.

Next, it's your turn to trace the ththth sound and write some of your own.

65

Lesson 52: Task 9
Writing sounds ch and p

Now we're going to practice writing the sounds you learned.

Tip: The ch sound uses the c sound and the h sound that we already learned to write. Let's put them together.

Watch me trace the ch sound. Trace the ch sound.
Next, it's your turn to trace the ch sound and write some of your own.

Now, watch me trace the p sound. Trace the p sound.
Next, it's your turn to trace the p sound and write some of your own.

Lesson 53: Task 9
Writing sounds w, v and p

Now we're going to practice writing the sounds you learned.

Watch me trace the www sound. Trace the www sound.
Next, it's your turn to trace the www sound and write some of your own.

W w w

w

Now, watch me trace the vvv sound. Trace the vvv sound.
Next, it's your turn to trace the vvv sound and write some of your own.

V v v

v

Lesson 53: Task 9 (continued)

Watch me trace the p sound. Trace the p sound.
Next, it's your turn to trace the p sound and write some of your own.

Lesson 54: Task 11
Writing sounds w and p

Now we're going to practice writing the sounds you learned.

Watch me trace the www sound. Trace the www sound.
Next, it's your turn to trace the www sound and write some of your own.

w w w

w

Now, watch me trace the p sound. Trace the p sound.
Next, it's your turn to trace the p sound and write some of your own.

p p p

p

Lesson 55: Task 10
Writing sounds ch and sh

Now we're going to practice writing the sounds you learned.

Watch me trace the ch sound. Trace the ch sound.
Next, it's your turn to trace the ch sound and write some of your own.

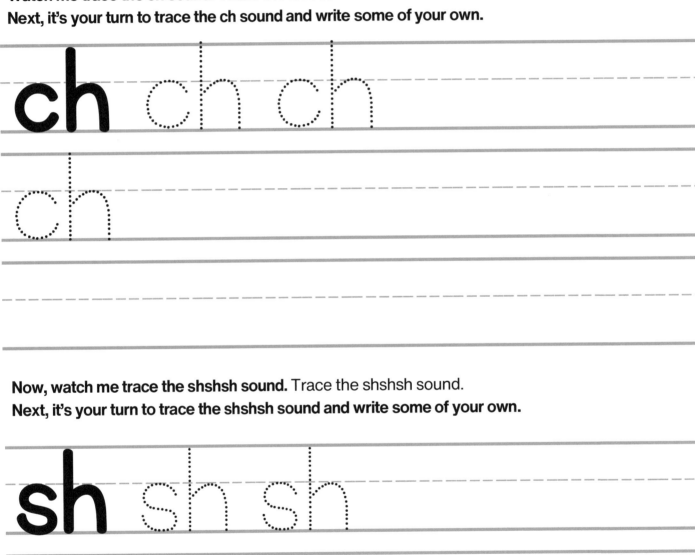

Now, watch me trace the shshsh sound. Trace the shshsh sound.
Next, it's your turn to trace the shshsh sound and write some of your own.

Lesson 56: Task 8
Writing sounds b and ch

Now we're going to practice writing the sounds you learned.

To write the sound "b", start at the dot on the top line and draw a straight line down vertically to the bottom line. Lift your pencil and draw a backwards "c" to the right of the line.

start here

step 2

Note: Point out to the child this sound takes up the whole line space instead of just the bottom.

Watch me trace the b sound. Trace the b sound.
Next, it's your turn to trace the b sound and write some of your own.

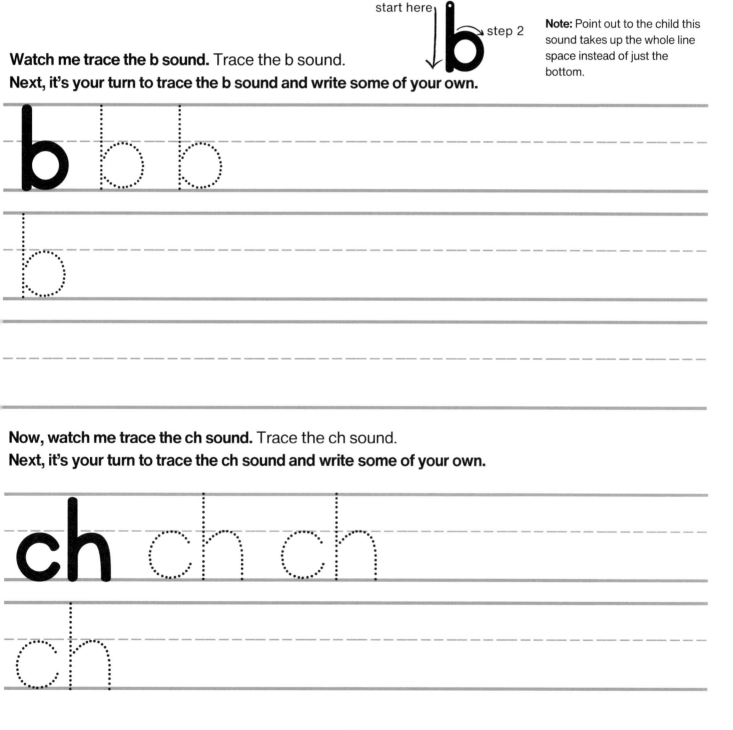

Now, watch me trace the ch sound. Trace the ch sound.
Next, it's your turn to trace the ch sound and write some of your own.

Lesson 57: Task 8
Writing sounds p and b

Now we're going to practice writing the sounds you learned.

Watch me trace the p sound. Trace the p sound.
Next, it's your turn to trace the p sound and write some of your own.

p p p

p

Now, watch me trace the b sound. Trace the b sound.
Next, it's your turn to trace the b sound and write some of your own.

b b b

b

Lesson 58: Task 9
Writing sounds d and b

Now we're going to practice writing the sounds you learned.

Watch me trace the d sound. Trace the d sound.
Next, it's your turn to trace the d sound and write some of your own.

Now, watch me trace the b sound. Trace the b sound.
Next, it's your turn to trace the b sound and write some of your own.

Lesson 59: Task 8
Writing sounds g and b

Now we're going to practice writing the sounds you learned.

Watch me trace the g sound. Trace the g sound.
Next, it's your turn to trace the g sound and write some of your own.

g g g

g

Now, watch me trace the b sound. Trace the b sound.
Next, it's your turn to trace the b sound and write some of your own.

b b b

b

Lesson 60: Task 10
Writing sounds v and g

Now we're going to practice writing the sounds you learned.

Watch me trace the vvv sound. Trace the vvv sound.
Next, it's your turn to trace the vvv sound and write some of your own.

v v v

v

Now, watch me trace the g sound. Trace the g sound.
Next, it's your turn to trace the g sound and write some of your own.

g g g

g

Lesson 61: Task 10
Writing sounds th and b

Now we're going to practice writing the sounds you learned.

Watch me trace the ththth sound. Trace the ththth sound.
Next, it's your turn to trace the ththth sound and write some of your own.

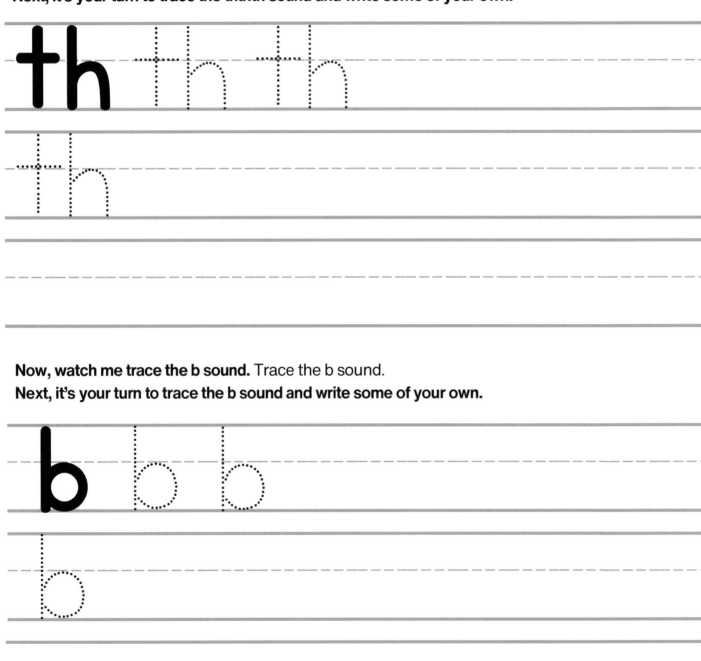

Now, watch me trace the b sound. Trace the b sound.
Next, it's your turn to trace the b sound and write some of your own.

Lesson 62: Task 12
Writing sounds y and w

Now we're going to practice writing the sounds you learned.

To write the sound "y", start at the dot on the middle line and draw a diagonal line down towards the right. Lift your pencil and draw a diagonal line down the other way and go past the bottom line.

start here

Note: Point out to the child this sound's "tail" dips below the bottom line.

Watch me trace the yyy sound. Trace the yyy sound.
Next, it's your turn to trace the yyy sound and write some of your own.

y y y

y

Now, watch me trace the www sound. Trace the www sound.
Next, it's your turn to trace the www sound and write some of your own.

w w w

w

77

Lesson 63: Task 11
Writing sounds y and b

Now we're going to practice writing the sounds you learned.

Watch me trace the yyy sound. Trace the yyy sound.
Next, it's your turn to trace the yyy sound and write some of your own.

y y y

y

Now, watch me trace the b sound. Trace the b sound.
Next, it's your turn to trace the b sound and write some of your own.

b b b

b

Lesson 64: Task 9
Writing sounds er and w

Now we're going to practice writing the sounds you learned.

Watch me trace the er (urrr) sound. Trace the er (urrr) sound.
Next, it's your turn to trace the er (urrr) sound and write some of your own.

Tip: The er (urrr) sound uses the e sound and the r sound that we already learned to write. Let's put them together.

er   er   er

er

Now, watch me trace the www sound. Trace the www sound.
Next, it's your turn to trace the www sound and write some of your own.

w   w   w

w

Lesson 65: Task 9
Writing sounds d and er

Now we're going to practice writing the sounds you learned.

Watch me trace the d sound. Trace the d sound.
Next, it's your turn to trace the d sound and write some of your own.

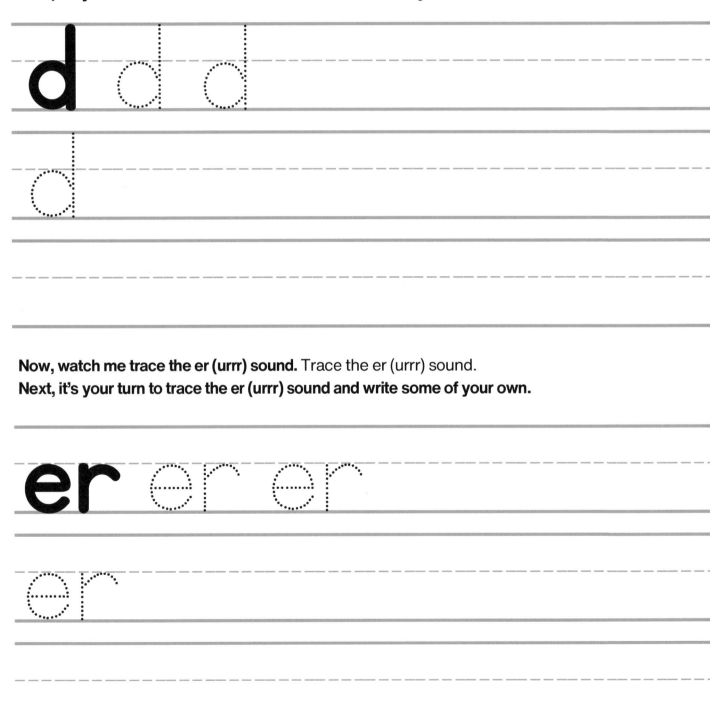

Now, watch me trace the er (urrr) sound. Trace the er (urrr) sound.
Next, it's your turn to trace the er (urrr) sound and write some of your own.

Lesson 66: Task 7
Writing sounds sh and y

Now we're going to practice writing the sounds you learned.

Watch me trace the shshsh sound. Trace the shshsh sound.
Next, it's your turn to trace the shshsh sound and write some of your own.

sh sh sh

sh

Now, watch me trace the yyy sound. Trace the yyy sound.
Next, it's your turn to trace the yyy sound and write some of your own.

y y y

y

Lesson 67: Task 11
Writing sounds b and p

Now we're going to practice writing the sounds you learned.

Watch me trace the b sound. Trace the b sound.
Next, it's your turn to trace the b sound and write some of your own.

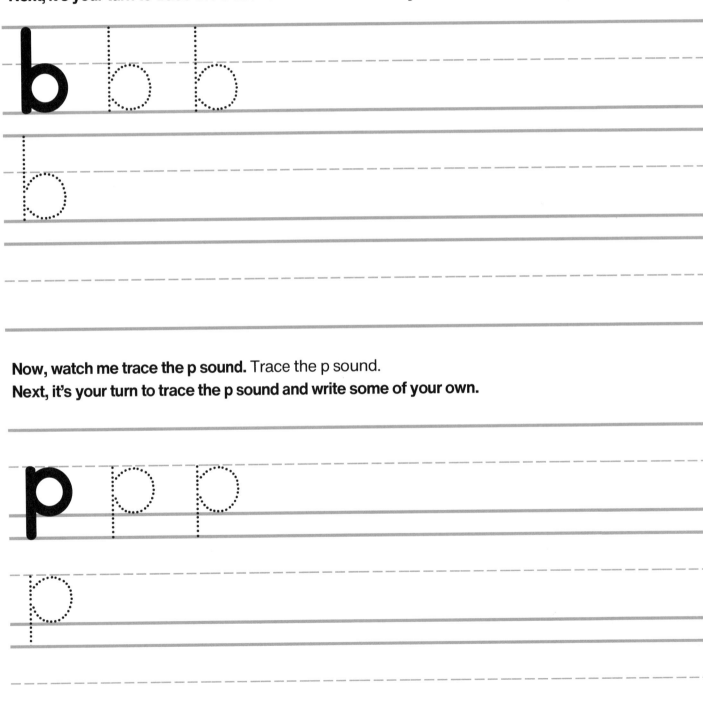

Now, watch me trace the p sound. Trace the p sound.
Next, it's your turn to trace the p sound and write some of your own.

Lesson 68: Task 9
Writing sounds j and er

Now we're going to practice writing the sounds you learned.

To write the sound "j", start at the dot on the middle line and draw a vertical line straight down past the bottom line and add a curve up to the left. Lift your pencil and add a dot.

Note: Point out to the child this sound dips below the bottom line.

start here

Watch me trace the j sound. Trace the j sound.
Next, it's your turn to trace the j sound and write some of your own.

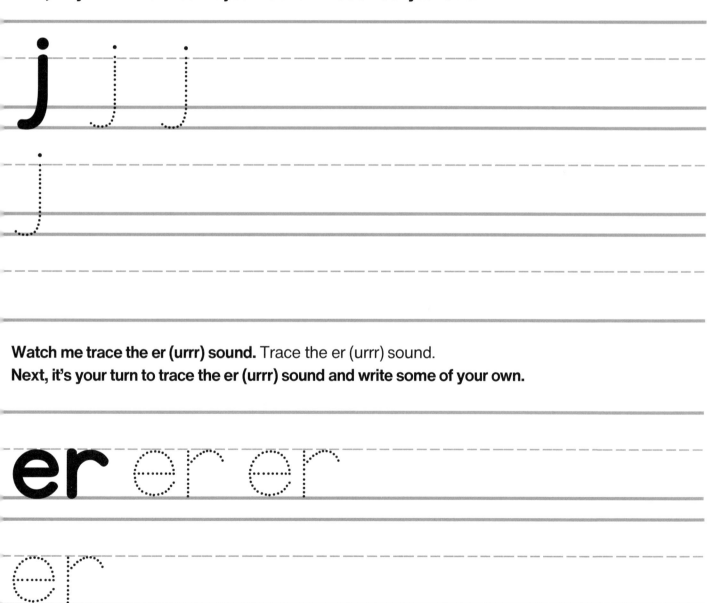

Watch me trace the er (urrr) sound. Trace the er (urrr) sound.
Next, it's your turn to trace the er (urrr) sound and write some of your own.

Lesson 69: Task 9
Writing sounds sh and d

Now we're going to practice writing the sounds you learned.

Watch me trace the shshsh sound. Trace the shshsh sound.
Next, it's your turn to trace the shshsh sound and write some of your own.

sh   sh   sh

sh

Now, watch me trace the d sound. Trace the d sound.
Next, it's your turn to trace the d sound and write some of your own.

d   d   d

d

Lesson 70: Task 8
Writing sounds w and j

Now we're going to practice writing the sounds you learned.

Watch me trace the www sound. Trace the www sound.
Next, it's your turn to trace the www sound and write some of your own.

W   w   w

w

Now, watch me trace the j sound. Trace the j sound.
Next, it's your turn to trace the j sound and write some of your own.

j   j   j

j

Lesson 71: Task 11

Writing sounds y and p

Now we're going to practice writing the sounds you learned.

Watch me trace the yyy sound. Trace the yyy sound.
Next, it's your turn to trace the yyy sound and write some of your own.

Now, watch me trace the p sound. Trace the p sound.
Next, it's your turn to trace the p sound and write some of your own.

Lesson 72: Task 9
Writing sounds wh and m

Now we're going to practice writing the sounds you learned.

Watch me trace the wh (www) sound. Trace the wh (www) sound.
Next, it's your turn to trace the wh (www) sound and write some of your own.

Tip: The wh sound uses the w sound and the h sound that we already learned to write. Let's put them together.

wh wh wh

wh

Now, watch me trace the mmm sound. Trace the mmm sound.
Next, it's your turn to trace the mmm sound and write some of your own.

m m m

m

Lesson 73: Task 9
Writing sounds n and b

Now we're going to practice writing the sounds you learned.

Watch me trace the nnn sound. Trace the nnn sound.
Next, it's your turn to trace the n sound and write some of your own.

n n n

n

Now, watch me trace the b sound. Trace the b sound.
Next, it's your turn to trace the b sound and write some of your own.

b b b

b

Lesson 74: Task 6
Writing sounds y and th

Now we're going to practice writing the sounds you learned.

Watch me trace the yyy sound. Trace the yyy sound.
Next, it's your turn to trace the yyy sound and write some of your own.

Now, watch me trace the ththth sound. Trace the ththth sound.
Next, it's your turn to trace the ththth sound and write some of your own.

Lesson 75: Task 6
Writing sounds w and y

Now we're going to practice writing the sounds you learned.

Watch me trace the www sound. Trace the www sound.
Next, it's your turn to trace the www sound and write some of your own.

W w w

w

Now, watch me trace the yyy sound. Trace the yyy sound.
Next, it's your turn to trace the yyy sound and write some of your own.

y y y

y

Lesson 76: Task 6
Writing letters x and ā

Now we're going to practice writing the letters you learned.

To write the letter "x", start at the dot on the middle line and draw a diagonal line down towards the right. Lift your pencil and draw another diagonal line down the other way, crossing in the middle.

Watch me trace the letter x. Trace the letter x.
Next, it's your turn to trace the letter x and write some of your own.

start here

X

X X X

X

Watch me trace the āāā sound. Trace the āāā sound. **Note:** Do not make the line over the **a**.
Next, it's your turn to trace the āāā sound and write some of your own.

Tip: The ā sound, even though it sounds different, looks just like the aaa sound when we write it.

a a a

a

Lesson 77: Task 9
Writing letters ū and b

Now we're going to practice writing the letters you learned.
What letters are on this page and what sounds do they make?

Tip: The ū sound, even though it sounds different, looks just like the uuu sound when we write it.

Watch me trace the ūūū sound. Trace the ūūū sound. **Note:** Do not make the line over the **u**.
Next, it's your turn to trace the ūūū sound and write some of your own.

Now, watch me trace the letter b. Trace the letter b.
Next, it's your turn to trace the letter b and write some of your own.

Lesson 78: Task 9
Writing letters x and er

Now we're going to practice writing the letters you learned.
What letters are on this page and what sounds do they make?

Watch me trace the letter x. Trace the letter x.
Next, it's your turn to trace the letter x and write some of your own.

X X X

X

Now, watch me trace the er sound with letters e and r. Trace the er (urrr) sound.
Next, it's your turn to trace the er (urrr) sound and write some of your own.

er er er

er

Lesson 79: Task 9
Writing letters z and s

Now we're going to practice writing the sounds you learned.
What letters are on this page and what sounds do they make?

To write the sound "z", start at the dot and make a horizontal line to the right. Then, make a diagonal line towards the bottom left. Finish with another horizontal line to the right.

start here

Watch me trace the letter z. Trace the letter z.
Next, it's your turn to trace the letter z and write some of your own.

Now, watch me trace the letter s. Trace the letter s.
Next, it's your turn to trace the letter s and write some of your own.

Lesson 80: Task 9
Writing letters u and z

Now we're going to practice writing the sounds you learned.
What letters are on this page and what sounds do they make?

Watch me trace the letter u. Trace the letter u.
Next, it's your turn to trace the letter u and write some of your own.

u

u

Now, watch me trace the letter z. Trace the letter z.
Next, it's your turn to trace the letter z and write some of your own.

z

z

Lesson 81: Task 10
Writing letters qu and x

Now we're going to practice writing the letters you learned.
What letters are on this page and what sounds do they make?

To write the sound "q", start at the dot and draw a circle. Make a slight vertical line up and then trace the vertical line back down below the bottom line, curling up towards the right to make a hook for the tail.

Watch me trace the letters q and u that make the kwww sound.
Trace the letters qu.
Next, it's your turn to trace the letters qu and write some of your own.

start here

Note: Point out to the child this sound's "tail" dips below the bottom line. We already learned how to write the u sound.

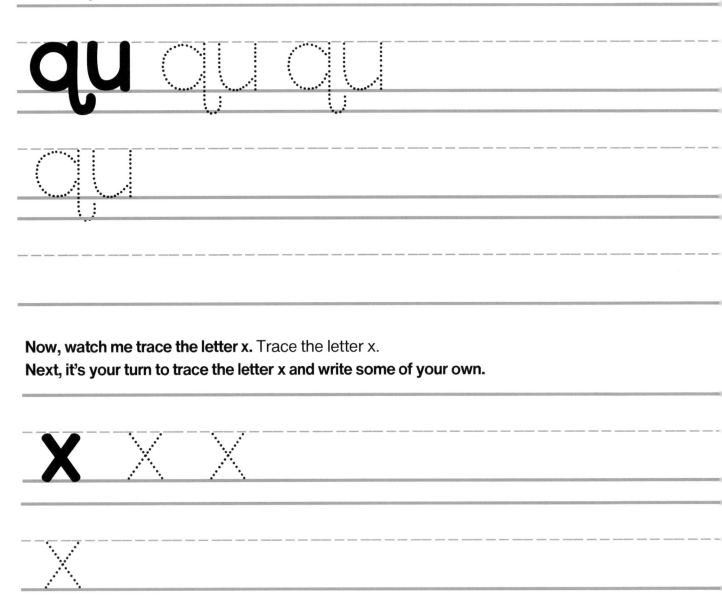

Now, watch me trace the letter x. Trace the letter x.
Next, it's your turn to trace the letter x and write some of your own.

Lesson 82: Task 10
Writing letters v and w

Now we're going to practice writing the letters you learned.
What letters are on this page and what sounds do they make?

Watch me trace the letter v. Trace the letter v.
Next, it's your turn to trace the letter v and write some of your own.

Now, watch me trace the letter w. Trace the letter w.
Next, it's your turn to trace the letter w and write some of your own.

Lesson 83: Task 10
Writing letters qu and z

Now we're going to practice writing the letters you learned.
What letters are on this page and what sounds do they make?

Watch me trace the letters q and u that make the kwww sound. Trace the letters q and u.
Next, it's your turn to trace the letters q and u and write some of your own.

Now, watch me trace the letter z. Trace the letter z.
Next, it's your turn to trace the letter z and write some of your own.

Lesson 84: Task 8
Writing letters j and t

Now we're going to practice writing the letters you learned.
What letters are on this page and what sounds do they make?

Watch me trace the letter j. Trace the letter j.
Next, it's your turn to trace the letter j and write some of your own.

Now, watch me trace the letter t. Trace the letter t.
Next, it's your turn to trace the letter t and write some of your own.

Lesson 85: Task 8
Writing letters th and d

Now we're going to practice writing the letters you learned.
What letters are on this page and what sounds do they make?

Watch me trace the letters t and h that make the ththth sound. Trace the letters th.
Next, it's your turn to trace the letters th and write some of your own.

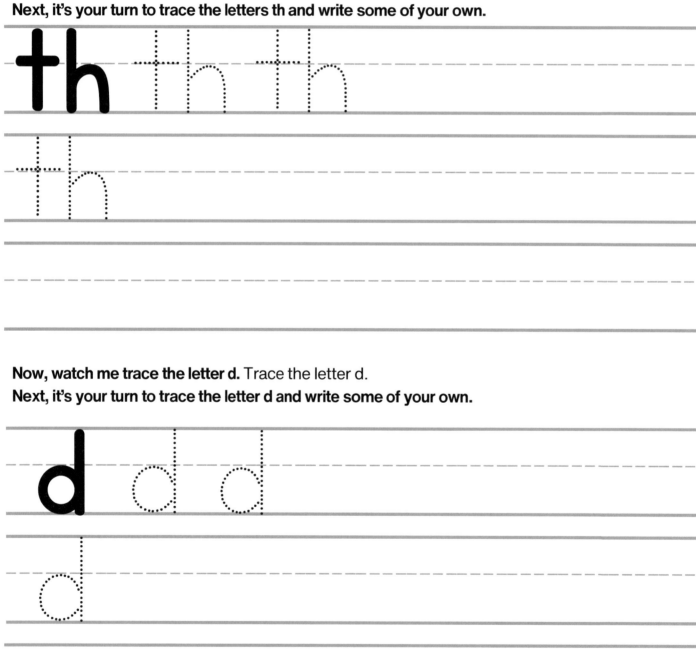

Now, watch me trace the letter d. Trace the letter d.
Next, it's your turn to trace the letter d and write some of your own.

Lesson 86: Task 8
Writing letters b and z

Now we're going to practice writing the letters you learned.
What letters are on this page and what sounds do they make?

Watch me trace the letter b. Trace the letter b.
Next, it's your turn to trace the letter b and write some of your own.

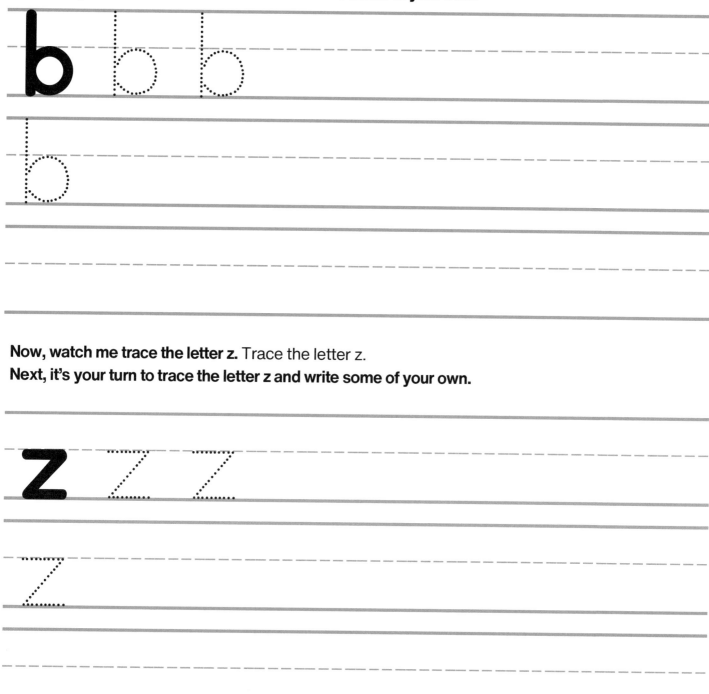

Now, watch me trace the letter z. Trace the letter z.
Next, it's your turn to trace the letter z and write some of your own.

Lesson 87: Task 9
Writing letters x and g

Now we're going to practice writing the letters you learned.
What letters are on this page and what sounds do they make?

Watch me trace the letter x. Trace the letter x.
Next, it's your turn to trace the letter x and write some of your own.

X x x

x

Now, watch me trace the letter g. Trace the letter g.
Next, it's your turn to trace the letter g and write some of your own.

g g g

g

Lesson 88: Task 9
Writing letters g and p

Now we're going to practice writing the letters you learned.
What letters are on this page and what sounds do they make?

Watch me trace the letter g. Trace the letter g.
Next, it's your turn to trace the letter g and write some of your own.

g   g   g

g

Now, watch me trace the letter p. Trace the letter p.
Next, it's your turn to trace the letter p and write some of your own.

p   p   p

p

Lesson 89: Task 8
Writing letters b and y

Now we're going to practice writing the letters you learned.

What letters are on this page and what sounds do they make?

Watch me trace the letter b. Trace the letter b.

Next, it's your turn to trace the letter b and write some of your own.

Now, watch me trace the letter y. Trace the letter y.

Next, it's your turn to trace the letter y and write some of your own.

Lesson 90: Task 7
Writing letters wh and e

Now we're going to practice writing the letters you learned.
What letters are on this page and what sounds do they make?

Watch me trace the the letters w and h which make the www sound. Trace the letters w and h.
Next, it's your turn to trace the letters w and h and write some of your own.

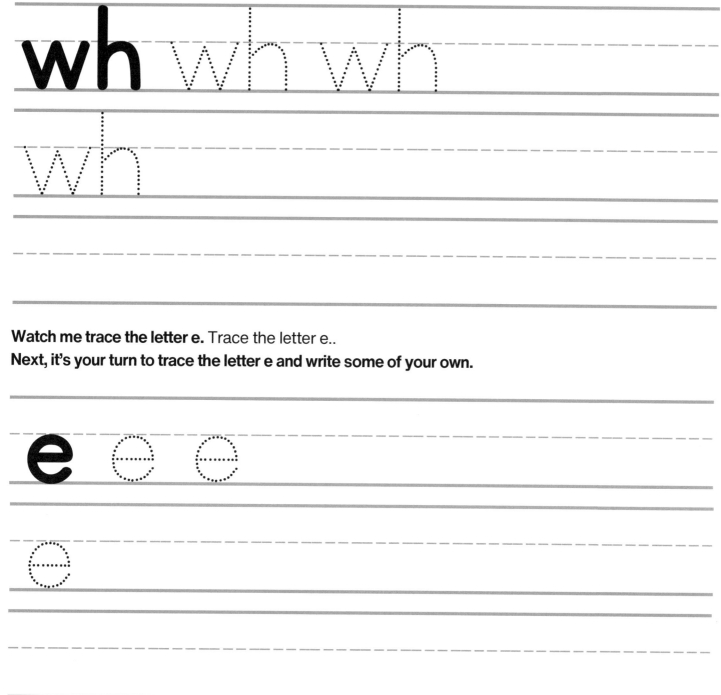

Watch me trace the letter e. Trace the letter e..
Next, it's your turn to trace the letter e and write some of your own.

105

Lesson 91: Task 10
Writing letters a and h

Now we're going to practice writing the letters you learned.
What letters are on this page and what sounds do they make?

Watch me trace the letter a. Trace the letter a.
Next, it's your turn to trace the letter a and write some of your own.

Now, watch me trace the letter h. Trace the letter h.
Next, it's your turn to trace the letter h and write some of your own.

Lesson 92: Task 8
Writing letters c and g

Now we're going to practice writing the letters you learned.
What letters are on this page and what sounds do they make?

Watch me trace the letter c. Trace the letter c.
Next, it's your turn to trace the letter c and write some of your own.

c c c

c

Now, watch me trace the letter g. Trace the letter g.
Next, it's your turn to trace the letter g and write some of your own.

g g g

g

Lesson 93: Task 6
Writing letters j and y

Now we're going to practice writing the letters you learned.
What letters are on this page and what sounds do they make?

Watch me trace the letter j. Trace the letter j.
Next, it's your turn to trace the letter j and write some of your own.

j   j   j

j

Now, watch me trace the letter y. Trace the letter y.
Next, it's your turn to trace the letter y and write some of your own.

y   y   y

y

Lesson 94: Task 8
Writing letters x and qu

Now we're going to practice writing the letters you learned.
What letters are on this page and what sounds do they make?

Watch me trace the letter x. Trace the letter x.
Next, it's your turn to trace the letter x and write some of your own.

Now, watch me trace the letters q and u that make the kwww sound. Trace the letters q and u.
Next, it's your turn to trace the letters q and u and write some of your own.

Lesson 95: Task 7
Writing letters qu and g

Now we're going to practice writing the letters you learned.
What letters are on this page and what sounds do they make?

Watch me trace the letters q and u that make the kwww sound. Trace the letters q and u.
Next, it's your turn to trace the letters q and u and write some of your own.

qu   qu   qu

qu

Now, watch me trace the letter g. Trace the letter g.
Next, it's your turn to trace the letter g and write some of your own.

g   g   g

g

Lesson 96: Task 7
Writing letters z and c

Now we're going to practice writing the letters you learned.
What letters are on this page and what sounds do they make?

Watch me trace the letter z. Trace the letter z.
Next, it's your turn to trace the letter z and write some of your own.

Z Z Z

Z

Now, watch me trace the letter c. Trace the letter c.
Next, it's your turn to trace the letter c and write some of your own.

C C C

C

Lesson 97: Task 6
Writing letters b and qu

Now we're going to practice writing the letters you learned.
What letters are on this page and what sounds do they make?

Watch me trace the letter b. Trace the letter b.
Next, it's your turn to trace the letter b and write some of your own.

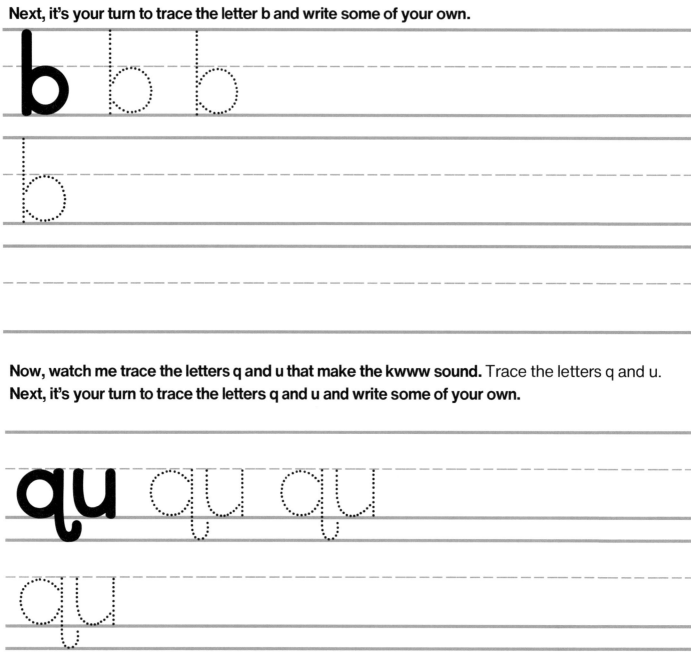

Now, watch me trace the letters q and u that make the kwww sound. Trace the letters q and u.
Next, it's your turn to trace the letters q and u and write some of your own.

Lesson 98: Task 6
Writing letters er and d

Now we're going to practice writing the letters you learned.
What letters are on this page and what sounds do they make?

Watch me trace the er (urr) sound with letters e and r. Trace the letter e and r.
Next, it's your turn to trace the letters e and r and write some of your own.

er   er   er

er

Now, watch me trace the letter d. Trace the letter d.
Next, it's your turn to trace the letter d and write some of your own.

d   d   d

d

Lesson 99: Task 6
Writing letters s and r

Now we're going to practice writing the letters you learned.
What letters are on this page and what sounds do they make?

Watch me trace the letter s. Trace the letter s.
Next, it's your turn to trace the letter s and write some of your own.

s s s

s

Now, watch me trace the letter r. Trace the letter r.
Next, it's your turn to trace the letter r and write some of your own.

r r r

r

Lesson 100: Task 6
Writing letters a and z

Now we're going to practice writing the letters you learned.
What letters are on this page and what sounds do they make?

Watch me trace the letter a. Trace the letter a.
Next, it's your turn to trace the letter a and write some of your own.

Now, watch me trace the letter z. Trace the letter z.
Next, it's your turn to trace the letter z and write some of your own.

Congratulations

Congratulations to both you and your child on completing all 100 lessons in the workbook. High fives all around!

Give yourselves a pat on the back for all the hard work and dedication you've put in. Seriously, you've both rocked it and should feel so proud. As you wrap up this workbook, just remember, this isn't the end of the road—it's just the beginning of a lifelong reading adventure.

There are tons of great ways to keep the reading momentum going. Hit up your local library for some new books that match your child's interests or have fun together labeling things around the house. Snag some letter magnets for the fridge or take turns reading bedtime stories. The sky's the limit!

Now go on and fill out your graduation certificate on the next page and display it proudly. Way to go super star!

Keep shining bright, and may your reading journey be filled with endless fun and learning.

CERTIFICATE
OF COMPLETION

This certificate is presented to the SUPER STAR

for completing 100 lessons of reading!

Date Completed

Instructor (signature)

Practice Sheet

Practice Sheet

Practice Sheet

Made in the USA
Columbia, SC
09 October 2024

44021477R00072